G000081359
Planet me

RIKU.POET

Planet Me

Contents

Hi, Riku here.
I just wanted to say a huge thank you for showing your curiosity and support in purchasing my first poetry book.

If you have time, your review would mean the world to me. Please follow the code below and share your thoughts. – Much love.

Why:

If someone were to ask me,
why is it that I write poetry,
I would tell them because it's about life to me.
A chance to speak and a moment to explain,
a pause to feel, a second to portray,
you can write in ways that speak aloud.
Deep emotions and feelings that can otherwise
enshroud.

If someone were to ask me,
why it is that I write poetry,
I would tell them that it's a chance to speak,
a moment to tell you all about me.
If you have ears to listen, a mind to learn,
come sit awhile and let me tell you of.

A life.

My life, that became something from
broken beginnings.
A failed attempt written off before the
first
transactions of oxygen,
replacing a cellular rich cocoon,
expelling fluid through lymph glands.
Sending...

A chain reaction of cellular
regeneration through
a body not yet ready and a set of lungs too small
too weak and too new,
to hold our air.

If someone were to ask me,
why it is that I write poetry,
I would tell them that is my chance to tell a story,
my story.
Of how I got from there to here -
of a scream so loud, they would hear.
And stop their medical proximation.
Baffled.
At how in the midst of the early 80's an unwanted
statistic suddenly became a medical miracle.
Leaving science pondering
how this could all be possible.
But yet "they"
in their earthly know it all wisdom,
slapped.
Me with a tainted label,
as a way to explain the unattainable
unexplainable mystery of how,
I stand here now.
As a testament to the wonders
of archaic Miracles.

Myself.

It takes but a moment,
to meet me where I am,
hiding in the open for
all.

Not loud brash or irascible,
but calm, quiet and
assiduous.

Small talk is simply wasted.
A drop of wisdom;
an ear of assistants.
Just take a moment sit and
listen.

Trusting kind and patients my virtue,
conversations all well-meant.
When vast understanding
and humble concern,
merit's honest opinion and care.

That is where you'll find myself,
smiling -
just over there.

It's there.

Up there just past
my grasp
I.
Can feel it,
envision it,
smile at it,
but then.
I drift again.
Into the depths
hoping that it'd
be there when I wake.
But "it" never is.

A brief flash of
vibrancy illuminating
the dark of my
mind's eye.
How words roll
endlessly through me
before,
I roll on over.
Blindfolded
to the
great beauty
and untameable

Beat from the wings
O
of creativity.
Lead by winds of
change.
I daren't sleep in case
I'll miss it.
And then, when I'm busy,
sometimes
it flies past.
With colour rich
stirrings
causing my heart to
jump.
Then comes
the time,
to sit and pen,
and I soon realise
that I'm chasing
rain drops.
Whilst craving an ocean.

Lucidity.

Did I write it?
I mean seriously,
did
I actually
write that poem,
about a really
unique ability?
Only a select
few have it?
Inspired by an event
I distinctly remember
reading about?
So, I dig in and search
notebooks turning
through
pages of penned
idioms.
Only then to discover
that.
I must have dreamt It.
An entire poem,
penned from
the comfort
of my mind.

Tiredness

There are times when
the day pulls me on
with no let up.
Seemingly careless
driven.
By the constraints of
the clock,
I struggle forward.
A vessel amongst thick
reeds.
My mind sluggish - unwilling
forgetting the simple.
Hoping to find a
glimmer of light within.
My darkened sojourned eyes,
for tiredness has gripped
again.
It's white hot tendrils
enveloping my being.
Now slows me too almost
useless.
My only outer sign,
is the dryness
of my eyes,
feebly masked by a smile,
of I'm fine.

Shards.

I’m a picture of whole
a mere dream,
Just out of reach.
Please hear me
listen.

A broken glass with many faces
slithers of misaligned
understandings.
Though grasped,
not fully quite yet mastered.
As rain falls upon a window
see how it makes a journey,
turning then roaming finding
its end?
Often then joined by another.

So here in my mind,
I’m one of the same.
Messages get scrambled
wires getting crossed
the short term loses
more often than not.

If plagued by a handful
of needed priorities,
I've learned to smile
whilst behind the façade,
I'm desperately trying
to remember the first.

A pen in my mind
has been my answer.
but by the time
I get down to paper,
it's gone, blown off course
lost again, deep within.

A grain of sand drowning in rain.

Then human interaction
a conversation between one,
- that I can do.
But when more than two,
I find myself standing
within a dust storm of noise
I'm lost, only I'm... smiling.

Time and time again conversation
turns between others,
leaving me stood looking
useless.

Whilst inside things
still have their meaning.

So if and when I do things
that appear so distant
random or odd.
Be assured that inside
I'm screaming and pleading
for my mind to work with you.

I honestly care for
all those I know,
and when I make mistakes
please know.
My tears flow
silent and broken.
A desperate wish,
that my mind of mirrors
could glint and shine.
Like yours.

Wax.

Moulded standing.
Not as you
but more like, me.
I balance
holding
weight over
my limbs of two.

Seemingly normal
not noticed until
I move.
Not like you
but more like, me.
As if gravity was
an enemy pulling
me down.

Taking all elasticity
turning it still.
as if porcelain
unyielding, laughable
undesirable.
Not like you
but more like, me.

Eyes look and wonder,
faces turn and frown.
A distain upon common
grace.
To those who
are.
Not like me
but more like, you.

Distance becoming,
within a room
now different.
Though surely
can't we all be the same?

Stereo typed
judged
mocked
belittled
scorned.
Whispers uttered
side glances veiled
by a slight of
of hand.

Received via
acknowledging nods,
agreeable to the
notion of.
Not like us
but more like, him.

Moving steadily
limbs that were
damaged.
Before life began
a scar, a tale
of a man.
Who didn't give in.

Desperately wishing
that they
were also made from wax,
So, as he could then,
mould and shape
To become
more like you
and less like,
me.

Dear memory.

Please can I ask you to remember things?
Like the time when I forgot to bring a pen?
Or
even the time to remember my meal in the oven?
Yes - it burned - no thanks to you.
So,

Dear memory.

Please can you remember the simple things?
As well as the more important ones?
Like,
he time where I forgot where I was?
Or what that person's name was?
You know - thingy with the hair?

Look I know you don't care,
but
I do- I really do.
You see,
You keep making a fool out of me.
Just last week or was it yesterday
when,
I overspent again?

You made me forget how much money I'd spent.
So please have a heart,
I'm trying my best so, could you?

How about we work together?

I'll do the life part, if you do the memory?

Kindest regards,
Me.

OH!
Now where on earth
did I leave my cup of tea?

Echoic memory.

Like a portal
peering through time.
Beckoning me to
step back into
significant moments
accented.
A sound.
Filed within my
mind categorised,
ordered – only
re-living when
that music plays.
Days, months,
exact times,
smells, faces, colours,
accurately formed.
Lessons to observe,
bad or good –
In this moment
my memory is perfect.
Just like I
wished it would
have always been.

Restless.

Hi ADHD.
Can you let me watch
a program or series?
Because right now I can't
seem make a single
choice.
As soon as I start one,
I'm bored.
Or I want to find one
that's,
Not even there.
So maybe a book,
But then.
I've three started,
unfinished.
Also, now I'm finding
-thanks to you,
I'm not in the mood
right now.
The thing Is, I'm restless.
Knowing I need
to rest yes.
But now I've got this itch,
to find a new book.

So here I am sat
with the tv on.
Several books on the
table whilst,
I google new novels
in genres of horror
wait.
I left my pasta,
boiling on the stove.
It's fine though,
I'll have a good meal to
watch a program with -
but seriously?
what should I
choose?

Cracks.

It’s
as if I’m upside
down.
Seeing the world
inversely.
Having been up
there.
So comfortable
but
now I’m not.
Knowing
or at least trying
to remind
myself.
It’s not what I do
now.
But rather,
how on earth
do I get
back up.?

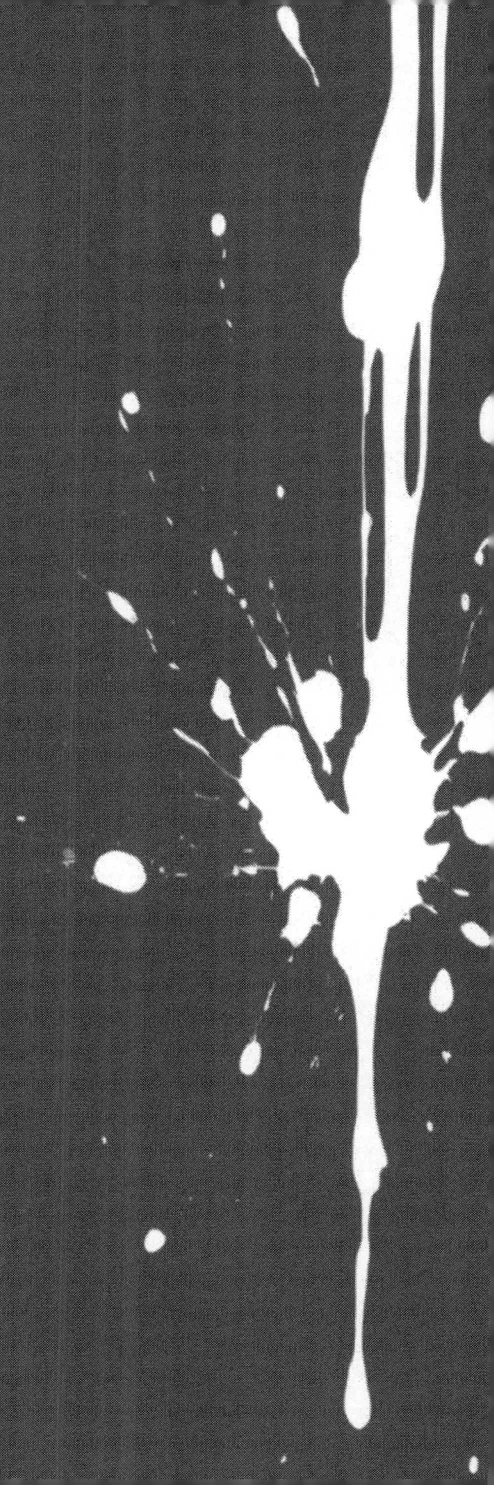

Iceberg.

How do I keep on going
masquerading as fine?
Painted; my face
so that outwardly
I'm smiling.
Though Inside silently,
I'm crumbling?
Worn my fingers to
the bone, feet insnared with
daily grit cutting
callouses.
Causing blisters to my heart strings
whilst flames lick white hot tongues
boiling my soul into fine vapours.
How to keep on dancing
this display of public
pretending perfection,
when inside silently.
I'm Crying.
My mind bent double
screwed into knots, holding.
A titanic of thoughts,
condensing and compacting
forming Icebergs; I'm waiting.
For the impending moment when
I.
Capsize.

The change.

Gone
simply implicitly
taken without warning.
Seemingly resolute in its
provocation of the present.
The application in when dealing
upon the co-incidental
opposition of the breaking of emotions.

No way of turning now,
In hope of unwinding the
frivolous hands
commanding the faces of time,
rather.
Held against the pinnacle.
A conjecture of personal obligation
weighing at their very nature silenced
at the voices of raw pain.

The road less travelled beckoning
excursion to the inquest.
Accepted now with infused momentum
casting shadows of well worn ideas
to the weary of mind and heart.
Is this the only way now?
Through forests of knives
and lava lit sky's.
Through outcrops of wrongs,

and heavy weighted yearnings
for the moments of old?

I force myself against desert heated winds,
ripping through glue shaped limbs,
from pages well-worn now
only torn.
Into new situations.
Forming obligations - not of my own,
but in directions stipulated.
From circumstances driven entirely
out of my control.

Surges.

If I could describe
to you what's
happening inside
of me.
It would be as if
I'm swimming within
the seas of turmoil
no life raft, or
view of land.
My limbs now
heavy with
weighted exhaustion,
the lure of succumbing
and becoming its
captor.
The creeping ever
closer to give up,
swallowing the
bitter waters of
weakness and failure,
sinking into piteous
self-prescribed loathing;
I cannot.
I
Must fight on.

Reoccurrence.

It seems to me,
that 11am is my
emotional flat-line.
If I start my day
well, awake feeling
light from the sun,
across my mind.
Then to wither as a,
rose parched in
summertime.

My colours lose
vibrancy as if
a rainbow at night.
Deep in my soul
now awash of self-imposed
apathy, stealing.
Life - for a time,
I then watch the
clock hands Tick.

Tick.

Tick.

Tock.

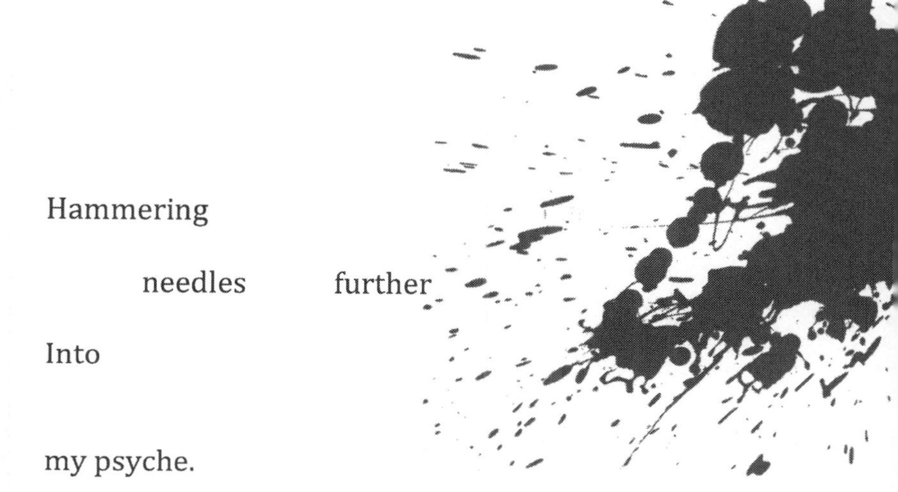

Hammering

needles further

Into

my psyche.

-I'm fighting.
Tears - holding back,
irrational ill perceived
emotions – as I drink,
the cup of pain.
Again,
again and again,
until it passes.

Ready for 11am
the next day.

Hero of nothing.

To carry
on being a hero; when I'm just,
some broken Porcelain.
Fragmented pieces now each crying,
in vein;
They bleed, dry.
My heart
torn to ribbons,
engulfed.
Within a tempest, laced with fine
salt.
Adding anguish to misery,
mocking my sanity;
wearing me as pride
upon the back of if only.
Here on the floor, my shards of empty-
I kneel.
Knowing it's just the turning of life.
As I try to pick up my soul
one small tear at a time.

Pressures:

I wanted today to finish.
Not to just be where I was
but to be able to stop.
I wanted to curl up and hide,
not caring about my left or my right,
the things in front or even the spaces left
beyond.
I just didn't want today to be a moment longer.
And then.
I let my own hand lightly grip my pen.
Etching slowly onto a scrap of torn
paper: thin,
my soul laid open.
Inside out now flowing,
allowing my being a moment in finding,
a pause.
To exhale; just breathe.
Whilst in that place, I came to realise;
that I am only
so very human.

Threadbare

Two threads; joined entwined
created intrinsically, unquestionably uniquely;
a life, this life; my life - called me.

Brokenness, the all seeing
hidden enemy,
held with vice-like gripped oppression -
sliced into pieces,
a once small delicate dream.

Now,
shards, carried on wings of pain
disillusion their destiny.

Life pulling;
changing
moulding, growing.
Becoming,
all the while
I;

A silent builder; learning to mask
a deep-rooted question
a haunting pain,
my face resembling that of another.

Years bring change;
part of a family,
who graciously,
wove me into a new song,
a song called Love.
Yet,

I.

Still masking;
becoming now the great pretender,
a daily masquerade.
Learning to dance with smiles
and forced brevity.
Things are all fine.
I don't feel, I'm ok.

Darkness now forcing my eyes
to widen when all others,
are in slumber.

Fear.

Fear of being alone.
Fear of never finding peace.
A place to feel like me on this journey called earth.

Fear the root; what if I speak?
What if I dare utter the motions of my heart?
A lost hurting soul,

adrift on the swells of
emotional turmoil?
Will I be left?
Cut loose, a thread
adrift?
An outsider; an
outcast?

Fear.

Years roll by, whilst all the while
emotions are just one step behind.
A haunting,
a ghost,
a mirror resembling the face of me.

People, places, faces,
cultures.
All with possible answers to my,
underlying pain
of,
where do I fit?

So, at last I turn and search,
staring ***fear*** in its face.
A plea to finally ask,
who are we?
To only discover that
time was indeed faster.

Ticking its last;
a thief that stole breath as its prize.

I.

was too late.

Too late to speak and then still, to listen.
Too late to ask and finally put to rest,
my inner turmoil.

The turmoil known as ghost.

Always standing just one step behind me.

So many questions
now with no answers.
Only pain as a reminder of how
fear held **me** back.

Through raw, broken and bleeding
strings,
my heart.
Now sings its melody.

Tear-stained eyes, I will no longer
allow a great pretending.
So I will let them fall,
with each drop, sing a new song;

mirroring two threads.
Once joined entwined
creating.
A hidden woven tapestry.
A face, a life, this life
called me.

I still feel you, though distance
has now become you.
A faint thread woven into my fabric
a memory, echoing
calling, whispering
reminding me
of you.

Laid to rest; now I grieve deeply.
Fear no longer, instead a thanksgiving.

Two threads;
though utterly useless and despised by some;
to me though,
a great and personal beauty;

To cherish and forever be,
your grateful,
proud,
and thread bare,
son.

Connections.

Standing in front
of the mirror,
reflected back at me,
are echoes
of you.
Silently I wonder
if you'd be
proud of me now.
My life lived
In ways I'd hope
to make you
smile.
Learning to get
back up after
many
a knock down
hardship and
trial.
I remember your
laugh,
the way you smiled
even,
the way your
hands
looked the same
as mine.

On that day when
we met again,
for you.
But for me
It was our first.
That day
now a captured
photograph.
Placed upon a mantle
a silent testimony
of you.
A piece of me.
Proudly held within
each breath,
accented by tears
I'm thankful -
not regretful
that you lived.
A deep pride
to be your son,
sharing in your
heritage
to wear now
as colours
telling a story
of your life,
for me.

To say goodbye.

When everything
within me
craves Hello.

To stand in silence
when so desperate
to hear your voice.
just
one
more time.

To have to let go,
when
my hands are
frozen closed,
at the cold
reality
of knowing
that I,
was too late.

Two lives
now laid still.

One son
wishing he
had one more
moment.

One more minuet
to be able to
hold you
in my empty
arms.

One more second
to say,
I love you.

The card.

Letters once written,
upon brightly coloured paper.
Seemingly simple in their
application,
a wish of good will;
a child's birthday card.
Meaningful for a moment,
until time passes by.

The card then, lay closed.
Silent and still.
Unbeknownst to the reader,
stored away with caring hands.
Waiting and yet;
holding within,
emotions to rival the greatest
love song.

Now.
Dust covered, almost forgotten,
still silent. Still waiting.
The words once again,
are finally uncovered and given
a freedom to light.

The card; written by a hand,
a life, a heart.
Reaches out as if warm tender
rays of love,
touching the void of a broken spirit.
whispering gently,
becoming words with power
to hold and to heal.

Once, just handwritten
upon a simple birthday card,
now;
A souvenir of a mother's
gentle embrace,
to a grown man.
Yet still; a small and lost,
hurting little boy.

Innermost

Time beginning.
Shattered into a million fragments,
before words even formed,
the insular cortex was silenced.
So young, so tender; so pure.
Trusting, longing calling for care, the basic human response denied.
Cocooned within a machine, lungs too new to move; a world of dark displayed.

Time ticking.
Yet still no response to a guttural cry
a mother's instinct washed away through a deluge of toxin,
a need to find feeling from her own bitter short comings.

Time moving.
Nursed now by another- not her.
Learning to find contentment by deflection.
Seeking independent consolation.
A wound forever deepening.

Time passing.
Placed in a family, given a life and love to grow,
Shards sticking together with Pritt-stick and plasters.
Guarded becoming secret, true nature untold.

Always living as if owing gratitude,
never quite belonging.

Time rolling.
Identity in question, skin divergent,
skills felt never good enough.
Losing the battle of indifference,
alone, misunderstood.

Time telling.
My heart now expertly hidden from years of pain,
reflected by warped imitations, a broken personality.
Caring whilst uncaring, not wanting to be touched.
Pushing boundaries, running from love desperately
yearning, a madman chasing the wind.

Time healing.
A new love found turning into a marriage, still not
quite fully let in.
My hidden core, left almost forgotten a bitter wound
only now haunting dreams.

Time reborn.
Now a father to a child of my own, emotions placed
deep within. A heart made paper thin.
Never to let go, always caring; a new piece of me.

Time retelling.
Wife still wanting to be let in, to be able to hold, touch
and kiss my broken fragmented heart.
Guarded, hidden, forgotten shown only a glimmer,
She waits.

Time freeing.
I suddenly see, reasons for hauteur. Deep wells now made clear, once only my reflection.
Showing me another, standing not leaving, hand holding mine, Seeing my very inner core.
My paper thin man-made heart, broken, shattered stuck with cheap plaster.
Now finally beginning to heal.

Rise.

Life begun,
invisible to the eye
and yet fully determined
woven together
with a majestic tenderness.
You grew as a seed
planted with care,
cocooned so gently within her.

Your soul then silently whispered
innocence,
the most precious of
virtues.
Dreams we birthed in hope for you,
plans made, spaces created
and Then.

Life took another turn.
No prayer or pleading would stop you
from sadly leaving our world,
our home we made -
just for you.

Now you rise full of colour
beauty and life.
Free to soar in perfect
harmony,
never to feel the pain

of leaving us behind or letting go,
but we.

Truly do.

I promise to try and live on,
daily.
Never forgetting but learning to
take small steps in memory
of you my dear child.

As I sit staring at our
memorial corner,
my tears still fall
but I know that one day,
I'll hold you – tight within my arms.
Just like we dreamed together,
though it won't be just for a moment-
but for all of an eternity.

Turmoil

If I just stopped to think,
even for a smallest little moment.
And tried to describe for you
my deepest true emotions,

It would be as if I'm lost
upon a tempestuous
white capped sea.
Adrift with no rudder,
no sail or compass leading.
Just huddled on a small deck
of a wooden vessel breaking.

Thrown rain with unmatched fury
from a howling violent wind.
Masking vision truth or clarity,
sucking life from every limb.

As Ahab's last lament
cried out,
before he went into
the depths,
I'm forced to bare a truer tale,
with knuckles white and breath
inhaled.

I scream for peace and tranquil
times,
whilst pulling at these thick chains
upon
cut and salted hands.

I'm a man who's had his fair share
from bearings cold embrace.
My tears are filled with grievance
As I seek out more life to chase.

Puppets.

I'm struggling.
really struggling.
Swimming against the tides
pulling me, dragging me down
holding me under walls of suffering.

My strings are broken,
not one but several broken.
Movements now staggered.
Once so smooth, now jilted, marred in pain.

Trying to stand
I need to lean against you,
for my strength is weakening
where will help come in my pleading
this wooden heart that's broken and bleeding.

The great pull of life, forever in motion,
I'm on main stage, bright lights shining,
reminding me, forcing me, turning me
spinning me into great knots.

I must keep on going.

Through gritted teeth and tear stained eyes,
I know I must. But I just need to lean.
Lean for support, lean for rest, lean to
mourn.

In one hand I hold these emotions,
these surging, raging emotions within
broken fingers and yet
in the other I have to hold the great pretend.

The great mask of perfect perfection,
hiding my true emotions.
Whilst mirroring the emotionless,
the greatest dance of life.

The dance called work and obligated responsibility.

Adrift floating

I; within the oceans of my heart,
the depth of which no man can fathom
wait.
I wait for a sign, that something
will lead me, show me a way through.
Only all I hear,
is the gentle rhythm of one.
And still I lay shipwrecked upon my very soul,
praying for a moment of weightlessness
to pull me on.
For I am drowning on the inside out.
I close my eyes and wish to fall, trusting you'll be
there to save me.
For I know,
deep down you are there.
In the silent places,
your voice is calling me.
And I you.

You.

With words so strong
you hold me.
Though I'm falling
you comfort me,
as light to dark
you guide me.

I'm lost,
within a maze
of my emotions.

I tumble at every
turn encircling.
Grief causing,
pain causing,
my bones
within my body
to ache.

I
desperately
ache.

Yet you
carry me.
Even when
I'm weighed down
to the lowest depths.

Your smile
radiates light upon
my darkest of night.
Holding out
your hands,
you silently draw
near.
enveloping my
wounds,
allowing me
at last a moment of rest.

To finally rest
just as I am.

Slowly,
together
you,
pull me
through.
Gently healing
whilst deeply
loving.

Me just
as
I am.

I needed you.
And you, were always right here.

Here.

You were utterly exhausted
and couldn't go another step
without crumbling to pieces
on the inside.
It's ok in those moments
to slow up and rest
letting life's lilted
pressures
lift from your chest.

So reach out your hand,
open your fist
and let me carry
these things
that seem to persist.
Stealing your smile at
life's little pleasures.
I'll set you free now,
as a bird with new
wings.

Metamorphosis.

Finding those
invaluable moments,
to access and then
extrapolate experiences
lived.
Lessons learnt
albeit all valuable.

Now to the souls
of those who are
otherwise forgotten.
A second chance, a moment
to sit, listen and lend
a cord once singed
in pain -now
entwined with
hope.

My battle torn
scars healed.
Having now the chance
in becoming perhaps
a form of medicine
for the
weary.

My tears now
worn as smiles.
My silence
transformed
to laughter.
As I remember that life
is one long
lesson to learn
and graduate.
Ultimately in the
act of selfless love,
for those
who lived first
without.

If I could.

I'd turn your shadows into
lanterns.
I'd take your fears
and mould them into wicks
igniting them with
hope.
I'd stand in the way of
your
shades of doubt
that crawl up behind
seeking to weigh you down
with the force of
depression.
And tear them apart
with my bare hands,
before swapping
a kaleidoscope of colour,
for your slate injected physiognomy.
You would be the brightest
person who'd walk the streets,
you would be my paper lantern
set free within a sea of others.

Expanding.

Moments in life,
feelings unhinged
misunderstood,
queried or even
labelled odd.
or - just plain lazy
finally,
as if a switch having been
flicked.
Shedding light onto a gift
not a curse, or
short fallings.
Heaviness now lifting,
held within arms of
relief - I'm not broken.
Just unique.

My brain is beautiful
purposeful and wonderful.

You.
May see things, experience
moments - plain unhindered
or even not bothered by.
Where as I.
Feel both externally and inwardly.

Whilst Your synapses fire in logical
expressions
my.
Brain plays with routes laughing
turning the everyday into a
playground of colour.
So, if I seem different
or branded with the 'not normal'.
Good.
I wouldn't want to be that now anyway.

For the first time,
I love who I am and will no longer
feel bad for it.
This new me, now ignoring
the what has been,
turning scars into life-lines.
Whilst eagerly
dreaming of new experiences,
becoming my new beginnings
crutched.
By a deeper understanding
now free of past failings,
breathing deeply with a
full knowing,
that I'm brilliantly different.

And that this is perfectly O.K.

To be a poet...

To be
a
Poet.

To be a craftsman taking words
placing words
selecting
words
as if they each
weigh immeasurable
amounts of value.
Bending rules, breaking
down
expression
In order to further express
to you a vibrant tapestry.

We. using only the finest
canvas and
purest
pigment,
paint.
we from our heart's intent on capturing
the perfect imperfect moment
between the
page
and

reader.

Having been dipped in unfathomable wells of vivid imagery,
Ignited in flames of emotional
ingenuity,
laid upon the great untameable stage
as if diamonds made from the purest of tears.
We.
Hope that each letter, each syllable,
each word,
serves its purpose
in conveying for you a story.
For each poetical verselet,
is a moment when "we" bare
our most open and raw emotions.
As
a
gift
freely
given.
To you and any who
take time to read it.

©Riku.Poet

Inhale.

Poems,
like silent whispers,
connect us through words
displayed In ways,
that make us feel
a little more
understood.
Visual representations
of emotions
held against limitations
hindered by the physical.
A mist they plead
for a way to reach
past heart strings.
The poetic release then,
as breath exhaled
sets in motion the telling.
Appearing first as mere ripples,
and yet contain the hidden power
of vast untameable oceans.

Those.

Today I'm gonna be.
For too long have I held my heart
cushioned in walls of solitude
too long have I;
In Fear of others
conformed.
Into a silent mirror of those
who aren't.

I've placed my quirks
taste
music
that I once wore proudly
high on the shelf of
young.
Why?

Should I grow older?
In a way that takes the colours of
me
turning them monochrome
for the simplistic
appeasement of
those who aren't?

So today I'm letting my
Inner hair loose.

I'm putting my
music loud,
smiling at my
reflection because
I am now
reflecting my
Inner true identity.

For too long I've let
those shoes collect dust.
But no longer,
for today,
this day

I will place them
back on my feet.
And step out
walking in light,
no longer in shadow
as the guy who,

has a theme tune
to his everyday.
Smiles at life
as he finds ways to play,
expressing an inner
desire to be,
creativity forever
free.

Printed in Great Britain
by Amazon

33665854R00040